PRACTICE LIKE YOU PLAY

Integrating Video Pitching Simulators Into Your Baseball Training Routine

Adam Battersby

Kent Press

Westport, CT

Kent Press
25 Poplar Plain Rd.
Westport, CT 06880
www.kentpress.com

This publication is designed to provide accurate and authoritative information regarding the subject matter covered. It is sold with the understanding that the publisher does not render legal, accounting, training, or other professional services. If professional assistance is required, the services of a competent professional person should be sought.

First Edition

ISBN: 978-1-888206-19-7

Dedication

Table of Contents

I.   Introduction

The purpose of this book is to explore the history of pitching and bowling machines for baseball, softball, and cricket; study the current market for such training devices; identify the pros and cons of such machines; and, finally, discuss and explain why video pitching simulators are a far better way to train hitters and batters for these sports for one, primary reason—they are the closest thing to training hitters and batters in a game-like environment.

This is not to imply that conventional pitching machines are not good training tools—they are. Furthermore, this does not suggest that players and coaches abandon using these machines—because they shouldn't. They have their place and are an effective way to train hitters and batters, but video pitching (or bowling) simulators are far better.

This book will show that while conventional pitching and bowling machines have many "pros," their "cons" can be detrimental to the development and growth of hitters and batters in all these sports. There is a "Better Way" to train young and experienced hitters for games. That better way is a Video Pitching (or Bowling) Simulator like the one designed, engineered, manufactured, and marketed by ProBatter Sports, where the hitter actually sees the video image of a baseball or softball pitcher winding up and releasing the pitch. That's coupled with a simulator that can throw any pitch that a live pitcher can throw at any speed to any location. The hitter can select either a right-handed or a left-handed pitcher, pitching from a full windup or stretch position. Visualization of the pitcher delivering the pitch makes it an authentic, game-like experience and fun to use.

Hitter's View of ProBatter Baseball Simulator

Batter's View of ProBatter Cricket Simulator

What enhances the player's experience with these video simulators is how easy they are to use—with a touchscreen controller. The player or coach can easily change the pitch settings or, when desired, allow the simulator to go into an "automatic" mode and deliver a pre-programmed sequence of different pitches to the hitter at different speeds and different locations—just like a pitcher will do in an actual game.

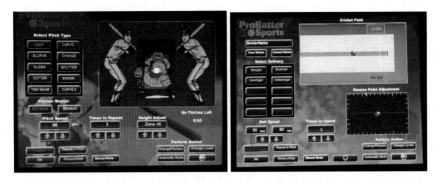

Touchscreen Controller for Baseball   Touchscreen Controller for Cricket

Performance during games is how players are ultimately judged and, in professional sports, what their salaries are based on. As with virtually anything, practice is critical, and practicing in a game-like environment is the best form of training possible. That is why, for example, NASA, the armed forces, and commercial airlines regularly use simulators to train astronauts and pilots who don't set foot into an actual plane or spacecraft until they have logged thousands of hours in flight simulators. It should be the same for athletes.

The last piece of the puzzle is a way to measure a hitter's performance, which can now be accomplished by using a ball tracking system such as the one marketed by Hittrax or Rapsodo. For example, the Hittrax system provides the following analytics:

- Exit Velocity
- Launch Angle
- Distance
- Point of Impact
- Play Outcome
- Strike Zone Analysis
- High-Speed Video w/ integrated metrics.

These metrics are measured while visually displaying the path of the ball on the simulator projection screen.

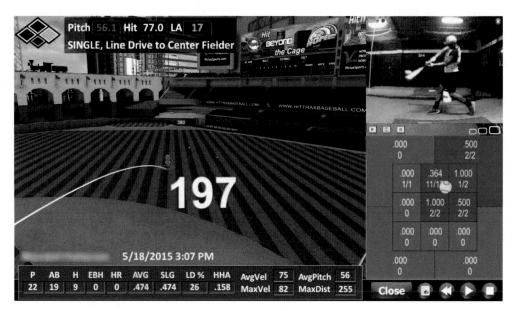

Projected Hittrax Display

II. Conventional Pitching Machines—The Pros and Cons

A. A History of Pitching Machines

Most everyone associated with baseball, softball, or cricket training has some familiarity with pitching machines for baseball or softball or bowling machines for cricket. They are the staple of everyone's training arsenal and have been used by virtually every player at all levels of the sport.

The Beginning

While they have become popular over the past half-century, the first pitching machine was invented in the mid-1890s when **Charles Hinton**, a mathematics instructor at Princeton University, found that his school's pitchers were getting sore arms from throwing too much during batting practice. In 1897, he first tried a catapult, which he admitted "failed altogether in point of accuracy of aim" and could not throw a curve. Realizing that wouldn't work, he designed a gunpowder-powered pitching device that was versatile, capable of variable speeds with an adjustable breech size, and could fire curve balls by the use of two rubber-coated steel fingers at the muzzle of the pitching machine.

The Princeton team tried using the device in practice, but the players were reluctant to get shot at, even with a baseball. Its first demonstration was

HINTON'S AUTOMATIC PITCHER.

in December 1896 when the Boston Beaneaters (later, the Boston Braves) came to Princeton to play an exhibition game. Boston's manager, Frank Selee, endorsed the machine, noting that when it was perfected, "the gun could be used to advantage early in the season before the pitchers' arms are strong." Not surprisingly, he didn't want his players to hit against it.

The following year, the machine was used in an intramural game between two eating clubs at Princeton. According to one account of the game, "There is but one serious defect in the operation of the machine, and that is the long time required for reloading. The frequent delays did not allow a full nine-inning game to be played." The machine was the subject of an article in *Scientific American.* The pinnacle of its fame came when it was used in a Southern Association game in 1900 when the gun struck out the first two batters and gave up no runs in two innings, with only one ball hit out of the infield.

While Hinton's mechanical "gun" was hardly a commercial success, inventors continued to pursue the idea. In 1908, a patent was issued on a "mechanical ball-thrower," and a similar device was described in *Baseball* magazine. Both machines used air-powered guns. Unfortunately, neither proved practical. Later decades saw unsuccessful attempts to create pitching machines using springs and even a trip hammer. In 1938, a pitching machine developed by St. Louis banker Byron Moser, which used what amounted to a giant rubber band, was demonstrated before a Cardinals game.

The Genesis of Commercial Units

Mechanical arm-pitching machines started appearing during World War II.

The first commercially successful mass-produced machine was the **Iron Mike**, whose prototype was built by Paul Giovagnoli in 1952. He ran a golf driving range near Topeka, Kansas, and wanted to add a batting cage, and when he could not find a satisfactory pitching machine, he built his own. Giovagnoli continued to improve his design and eventually opened his own company, Master Pitching Machine, which still operates.

Iron Mike Pitching Machine

While the mechanical arm-type pitching machine popularized by the **Iron Mike** machine dominated the market for many years, wheel-type machines quickly overtook them where balls were delivered through a pair of rotating wheels, which generally required fewer moving parts and were less expensive to operate, plus they could be made portable.

Larry Ponza was the inventor of the first portable, on-field pitching machine, called the **Power Pitcher**, which pioneered its use in Little League in 1952. From then until 1992, he continued to develop and patent several different pitching machines, a batting practice device, and an automated batting cage with the **Athletic Training Equipment Company ("ATEC").**

Larry Ponza's Power Pitcher

Kester's Curvemaster Machine

It wasn't until the late 1960s that a pitching machine could repeatedly throw curveballs—that was accomplished by J.C. Kester with his **Curvemaster**.

In 1970, John Paulson set out to build a baseball pitching machine to help his two sons become better hitters. He began investigating the various pitching machines available at the time but found them lacking in many aspects, e.g., they were prone to falling apart under regular use, too heavy and hard to move, could not throw strikes consistently, or would not throw realistic curves. Paulson purchased a patent for the use of pneumatic tires to throw baseballs. He later incorporated some ingenious ideas to create a new pitching machine. This machine not only threw all types of

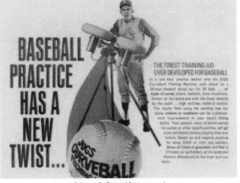

Jugs Advertisement

pitches—curves, sliders, fastballs, and even sinking split-finger fastballs at any speed desired—but it was also durable, trouble-free, and light enough to be transported in the trunk of a small car. The machine was named the **JUGS Curveball** Pitching Machine, from the old-time baseball expression "jug-handle curve."

In 1973, **Automated Batting Cages** ("ABC") introduced the first wheel-style commercial machine for batting cages. In 1980, they developed the first Master Control Panel for batting cages to operate all machines centrally in a facility. Later, they invented the first dimple-style urethane, baseball, and softball for use in a batting cage.

For the remainder of the 20th century, these four companies dominated the pitching machine market. However, new companies such as BATA, Heeter,

Original ProBatter Video Simulator

and First Pitch marketed other two-wheel machine units.

The pitching machine market changed dramatically in 2000 when **ProBatter Sports** introduced its P-100 video pitching simulator, which employed a three-wheel pitch head rather than the traditional two-head machines and computer controls. Adding the third wheel allowed the machine to throw curveballs and screwballs without changing the head's position. Computer controls allowed the machine to change positions and throw different pitches quickly. The ProBatter unit was so revolutionary that it was the subject of 13 U.S. Patents and a raft of international patents.

ProBatter's Original 3 wheel Pitch head

Home Plate Machine

While the ProBatter simulator incorporated a video projection screen, the pitching machine industry quickly recognized the advantage of adding a third wheel. It began incorporating a third wheel for conventional, non-video pitching machines. A few years after ProBatter's introduction, **Sports Tutor** began selling its Home Plate machine, which used three wheels, computer controls, and ProBatter's patented braking system. Unfortunately for Sports Tutor, it was found to have infringed ProBatter patents, and after a trial, the court found in favor of ProBatter.

Over the next ten years, **JUGS** and **ATEC** introduced their own computerized, three-wheel machines.

Jugs 3-wheel machine

ATEC 3-wheel machine

Newcomers, **Sports Attack,** with its line of **Hack Attack** machines, **Rawlings,** and machines by **SpinBall,** have all entered the market with lines of computerized three-wheel machines.

Cricket Too

In 1985, a club cricketer, Michael Stuart, invented the first cricket bowling machine named the "**Bola Machine**," which used a microprocessor to adjust the machine in 1-mph increments. Over the years, the line of Bola machines became the industry standard for conventional non-video cricket bowling machines, and robotics in the cricket bowling machine has seen drastic and dynamic advancements.

Bola Cricket Machine

A programmable bowling machine called **Merlyn**, built by Henry Pryor, a British cricket coach which claimed to be able to "bowl any ball known to man," received much public attention when it was used by the English cricket team in the run-up to and during the 2005 Ashes series.

One-wheel, two-wheel, and three-wheel cricket bowling machines are now available for various uses, including entertainment and training purposes and propulsion devices, e.g., rotating wheels, pneumatics, and spring-actuated throwing devices.

Crick Attack Machine

Sports Attack's **Crick Attack** machine was the first machine to bowl seam, swing & spin without requiring significant adjustments to the head unit between deliveries disguised and existing as an advancement. Leverage Cricket Bowling Machine's **Leverage Winner** was the first computerized two-wheel cricket bowling machine with robotic alignment amalgamated with digital and P.C. operations.

Again, **ProBatter** led the way in the area of video bowling simulators with the **Pro-Batter PX2 Cricket Video Simulator,** which relied on input from the England

ProBatter Cricket Simulator

and Wales Cricket Boards (ECB) and has been used by a number of the national teams and ICC Training Centers.

B. The Pros & Cons of Conventional Pitching Machines

The Pros

Everyone who has played baseball, softball, or cricket has, at one point or another in their lifetime, hit or batted against a pitching machine, whether in a batting cage, training center, on the field, or in their backyard. They are the staple of training equipment for these sports.

While they offer numerous advantages for players, they can't help them independently develop skills they may lack, e.g., confidence at the plate, consistency, hand-eye coordination, etc. While these skills can all be developed by facing live pitching, the reality is that the vast majority of players don't have the luxury of being able to face actual pitchers. Even when they do, the type or caliber of the practice pitcher may be of a lesser quality than they would face in an actual game.

Pitching machines give hitters more "reps" and allow them to work on their swing. They can also help players learn to hit curveballs, which almost every player finds challenging. A pitching machine can significantly help a young player develop plate techniques and skills and help them improve their stance, posture, and position at the plate.

Similarly, pitching machines are an excellent way to help batters perfect their hand-eye coordination. Batting coaches regularly use pitching machines to work with hitters struggling with a particular pitch or location. Taking batting practice against a machine that throws the very pitch that a hitter would struggle with during a game is an excellent way for the hitter to overcome that weakness.

Finally, pitching machines are helpful for hitters to practice their timing since they throw the same type of pitch at the same speed to the same location, thus allowing the hitter to practice against that pitch. If the hitter needs to work on fastballs just outside the strike zone, the machine can be set to throw that pitch repeatedly, and the hitter perfects that skill with that pitch.

The new 3-wheel pitching machines on the market, complete with more sophisticated computer controls, have overcome many limitations of the older single-pitch pitching machines typically found in batting cages.

The Cons

Many of the same advantages that make conventional pitching machines excellent training tools are also why they can harm a player's development. The reason is simple: Timing. **HITTING IS ALL ABOUT TIMING!** This is particularly true as pitchers start throwing harder and faster and begin to change the type and location of the pitches. Hitters are regularly taught to WATCH the pitcher in a game, time their windup, and focus on the release point of the pitch. This allows the hitter to be ready for a pitch and successfully hit it.

The problem with conventional (non-video) pitching machines is that there is no visible pitcher to time before the ball is released. With some units, the hitter may be forced to

Sleeve Feeder for Pitching Machine

time the pitch by watching a ball roll down a tube before entering the machine. This is particularly true in most batting cages, which rely on an automatic feeding system for their pitching machines.

In other cases, a light may appear on the pitching machine, warning the batter or hitter that the ball is about to be delivered.

Where non-video machines are used in tunnels or on the field, a coach may hand-feed the ball into the machine, alerting the hitter to a coming pitch by holding up the ball before dropping it into the machine.

Coach Hand Feeding Ball

THIS IS NOT THE WAY to prepare hitters or batters for a real game.

It should, therefore, come as no surprise that when some coaches rely on conventional pitching machines, mainly single-pitch machines, to train their hitters, they are disappointed with their player's performance in subsequent games. The reason is simple—such machines throw off the hitter's timing for a real game.

This problem is exacerbated when a commercial batting cage uses a "short" cage, i.e., less than the standard distance between the mound and the plate. That is certain to throw off the hitter's timing.

III.   Video Pitching Simulators— What Are They?

A.   Introduction

Video pitching simulators are simply the current generation of pitching machines, combining a computerized pitching machine with a video display that allows a hitter to see a video of an actual pitcher winding up and throwing a pitch. Hitting is all about timing for a hitter or batter. They "time" the delivery of a pitch based on the pitcher's motion and windup.

Combining that visual aspect of the pitcher winding up and delivering a pitch with the delivery of the pitch allows the hitter to better prepare for the

ProBatter PX3 Video Pitching Simulator in Action

pitch. With conventional pitching machines, the best the hitter can do is to watch a ball roll down a chute or a coach signal that a pitch will be delivered. With a video simulator, the hitter can time the pitch and observe arm angles and release points to help differentiate the type of pitch being delivered. This is particularly important for the older players, who will face pitchers in games who throw different pitches at different speeds. Pitch recognition is essential to hitting, and video simulators assist the hitter.

B.   Video Pitching Machines (Not Simulators)

The incorporation of video images with conventional pitching machines first entered the market in the 1990's. The concept was described in U.S. Pat. No. 5,195,744, issued in 1993 to Neil S. Kapp et al. for Baseball Batting Practice Apparatus with Control Means that combined a video projection system with a conventional pitching machine manufactured by Pacer Manufacturing Co.

The patent was eventually licensed to a Georgia-based company called The MIR Corporation, which introduced a video pitching machine that combined a projected video image of an actual pitcher and a conventional pitching machine. The unit was primarily used for entertainment purposes. Because the pitching machine could not throw different pitches, the hitter knew the pitch type and where it would be delivered.

The MIR machines were used at several MLB All-Star games as part of their Fan Fest, were generally enjoyed by all, and were licensed for use in other countries, including Japan.

Typical Japanese Batting Cage

Japanese batting cages have long used video screens with conventional pitching machines. These machines are similar to the MIR machine and, as was the case with the MIR machines, were primarily entertainment products and not video pitching simulators since they could not "simulate" the actual pitches that a pitcher would throw in a game. While they were an improvement over conventional non-video pitching machines, they did not rise to the level of an actual simulator.

Indian Cricket Simulator

Similarly, some video pitching machines have been used in South Korea's batting cages, such as Screen Baseball at **Strike Zone** in Jonggak. Again, these are video fronts for conventional, single-pitch pitching machines.

Since 2016, **Straight Drive** Sports & Leisure from India has marketed their Straight Drive automatic video cricket simulator in India and other cricket-playing countries, and it has been generally well received based on market penetration.

Batfast Video Game

Some other video pitching machines have entered the market, primarily applicable for entertainment. One such product is **Batbox,** which is intended for use at entertainment or hospitality venues, restaurants, or sports bars.

Similarly, **Batfast** has introduced a series of sports-oriented, live video games for various sports, including baseball and cricket.

Finally, there are some "virtual" pitching simulators where a video image of an actual pitcher is displayed, and a hitter tries to hit an imaginary virtual reality pitch using a headset. One Company that markets such products is **WIN Reality**.

Virtual Reality Simulator

C. The Advent of Video Pitching Simulators

The first actual video pitching simulator was introduced in 1999 by Pro-Batter Sports when it displayed its ProBatter Professional unit at the Baseball Trade Show at the MLB Winter Meetings in Anaheim, CA. It was the first video simulator that combined a projected image of an actual pitcher with a computerized pitching machine that could throw different pitches at different speeds to different locations—just like a pitcher does in a real game. The ProBatter Professional unit was unique because it was designed and engineered specifically for the task, not a combination of different components produced by different manufacturers.

An Early ProBatter Video Simulator

The 1999 ProBatter Professional had been beta-tested with the Boston Red Sox and the Jim Lefebvre Training Center before its introduction. It would ultimately become the subject of and protected by thirteen U.S. Patents and several corresponding international patents.

The original ProBatter Professional simulator would later evolve into three subsequent generations of simulators, each incorporating current technology and offered at lower prices. The first ProBatter was introduced at a price point of $95,000, while the current generation of ProBatter simulators, the PX3, is at a price point of $27,495, about a quarter of its original price point.

Since ProBatter introduced the Professional in 1999, some video pitching simulators have hit and been removed from the market. The first was a simulator called **Abne**r by a company called Fastball Development. That simulator, introduced in 2003, was also a dedicated simulator rather than the video conversion of an existing pitching machine. It had some interesting features, including a variable release point. Rather than a video image per se, it used LED lights. The Abner simulator had a price point of $165,000 and, unfortunately, did not last long—less than three years on the market.

Other manufacturers have tried to create video simulators by marrying a video display unit and another party's pitching machine. Still, no one has tried manufacturing and selling a complete video pitching simulator until recently when a Canadian company introduced a video simulator called **Trajekt**, which purports to simulate the images of actual MLB pitchers and their pitch sequences. The

The Canadian Trajekt Simulator

product has been leased to MLB teams for multi-year, six-figure, annual lease payments—a price point that has limited their market penetration, even at the MLB levels.

Finally, several ball-tracking products are marketed as "simulators," although they don't otherwise fall into the category of video pitching simulators. For example, **Hittrax** and **Rapsodo** are excellent ball tracking systems that provide the hitter with analytics about the ball that was hit and even track it on a

Batting Cage with Hittrax System

computer or projection screen to demonstrate the path of a ball. They are excellent add-ons to true video pitching simulators to ultimately create a "Smart Cage," as will be explained later in this book.

IV. ProBatter Sports—The Industry Leader

A. Background

Since ProBatter Sports introduced its first simulator for baseball in 1999, it has been the industry leader in video pitching simulators.

The underlying idea for the current line of products came from Greg Battersby, an intellectual property attorney and former baseball player and youth coach. In his hometown of Westport, CT, he coached several youth league teams and players, where he trained hitters, including his sons, for many years, using a batting cage and JUGS pitching machine in his backyard. Mr. Battersby quickly observed the limitations of machines that repeatedly threw only a single pitch at the same speed to the exact location.

In 1997, he and his law partner, Chuck Grimes, conceived the concept of a three-wheeled pitchhead. Working through a commonly-owned company, Kent Communications, they assembled a team consisting of a mechanical engineering professor to perform the necessary engineering studies, a machine design firm to design and prototype a working unit, and a computer programmer to develop a control system to facilitate the operation of the machine. They added an audio-visual expert to create a video front that would let hitters see an actual pitcher's image and time their release.

By 1998, they began testing the first generation of the ProBatter simulator at a commercial batting cage in Connecticut, where local hitters put the

Red Sox Facility in Ft. Myers

system through its paces. Enthusiasm was high at the facility, and in 1999, representatives from the Boston Red Sox were invited down to see the system in operation. They were sufficiently impressed and invited Kent to bring a unit down to their training facilities in Ft. Myers, FL, for use by their top prospects during the 1999 Fall Instructional League. The machine was well received, and Kent obtained some valuable feedback and recommendations.

B.   First Simulator Introduced in 1999

Buoyed by their experience with the Red Sox, the founders formed Pro-Batter Sports, LLC. They formally introduced the simulator to the public at the Baseball Trade Show, which was held in conjunction with the 1999 Major League Baseball Winter Meetings in Anaheim, CA. The Company sponsored

1999 Baseball Trade Show in Anaheim, CA

the opening night reception and installed a working batting cage in the middle of the reception hall. The Pro-Batter simulator was the "hit" of the show, with several MLB teams expressing serious interest in the equipment. Players, former players, and coaches were universally excited about the equipment, and at least one Hall of Fame player said, "If I had one of these, I would have hit .400 five years in a row."

Following the Baseball Trade Show, the current entity, ProBatter Sports, LLC, was formed, and it embarked on an accelerated engineering program to address some of the suggestions offered by the players during the Fall Instruc-

tional League and at the Trade Show. By May 2000, the design of the original ProBatter Professional baseball simulator was completed, and units were successfully beta-tested with the New York Mets at Shea Stadium and the Boston Red Sox at Fenway Park. A unit was also subjected to fatigue testing, where it was successfully run for more than 250,000 pitches. Beta field tests were

Shea Stadium in NYC

also conducted at various commercial training facilities, including one in Mesa, AZ, run by former Major League player Jim Lefebvre, to test its ability to withstand the rigors of a training environment and the Company's abilities to service the equipment at a remote location. Once again, the equipment passed with flying colors.

By the end of 2000, the Company began shipping the Professional baseball simulator units to selected "early adopters" of the equipment.

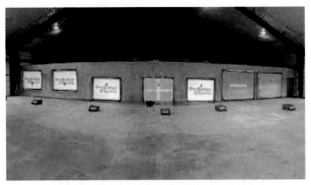

Typical Batting Cage with ProBatter Simulators

Since that time, ProBatter has manufactured and installed more than 600 video simulators throughout the United States and in 7 international countries. Customers have included the New York Mets, New York Yankees, Cleveland Indians, Chicago White Sox, Los Angeles Dodgers, and Pittsburgh Pirates, to name a few. Also, simulators have been sold to and installed at top college programs, including the University of Florida, the University of Maine, Ohio University, Ohio State University, the U.S. Naval Academy, and Angelo State University. In 2004, the Company installed a unit in Japan with the Chiba Lotte Marines of the Japanese Professional League, and a unit was sold to the Chinese National Baseball team. Since its inception, more than 250 commercial batting cages and training facilities have purchased video simulators.

C. Development of Related Products

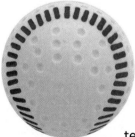

ProBatter designed and patented a seamed urethane baseball and softball, which they licensed to Baden Sports. In the batting cage market, these balls have become the most commonly used pitching machine balls (for baseball and softball).

Seamed ProBatter Ball by Baden Sports

In 2001, ProBatter Sports introduced its ProBatter II line of products, including video conversion kits for conventional ATEC and Iron Mike single-pitch pitching machines. The ProBatter II line permits one to inexpensively upgrade their existing equipment into video tunnels for a fraction of the Professional line of multi-pitch simulators.

In 2002, ProBatter developed its first Tunnels to Go® mobile batting cage product, which mounts an Iron Mike pitching machine and a ProBatter II video conversion kit in a trailer. A Professional version of the Tunnels to Go product was introduced in 2004, incorporating a ProBatter Professional pitching simulator in a trailer.

ProBatter PX3 Simulator

Since its first video pitching simulator in 1999, ProBatter has developed and introduced three subsequent generations of top-of-the-line, multiple-pitch simulators,

ProBatter's Challenger

the current being the PX3 video simulator, which was introduced in 2021. Each new generation of simulators has more features than the previous one at a significantly reduced cost. One of the primary features of the PX3 is its easy-to-use touchscreen controller, which allows a player or coach to change speeds, pitches, or locations easily.

In 2022, ProBatter also introduced a non-video version of the PX3 simulator called the Challenger, which uses the same pitch head as the PX3 without the video projection system. It can be upgraded to a PX3 video simulator by adding the video projection system.

Strike Out Pro Pitcher Trainer

In 2018, ProBatter introduced the first video training product for pitchers, the Strike Out Pro™. This novel pitcher training product permitted pitchers to practice against video images of actual players while measuring their ability to hit spots in the strike zone with various pitches at different speeds. At the end of each session, the pitcher (and his coach) would receive a computer printout of the session and his ability (or inability) to achieve his goals. That year,

Strike Out Pro Pitcher Trainer

ProBatter's Strike Out Pro pitcher trainer received a Best in Show award at the annual ABCA Coaches meeting.

The Combo Units

One of the most popular PX3 units is the "combo" unit, which stacks two versions of PX3 simulators, e.g., baseball/softball, baseball/cricket, etc., behind a projection screen. They share the same controller, projection system, and touchscreen controller. This allows customers to use the same tunnel for two sports by simply switching from one version to another with the touch of a button. Imagine the real estate you can save using a single tunnel for two sports.

Combo Unit

Reorganization of ProBatter Sports

In 2023, ProBatter Sports underwent a corporate reorganization, forming a partnership with Virginia-based eCMMS, a subsidiary of Foxconn, the world's largest technology manufacturer and service provider, to produce its line of pitching and bowling simulators. Foxconn is the principal supplier to Apple. This was done to meet the growing demand in the United States and abroad.

Advancing Through Innovation

As a part of its new relationship, ProBatter has begun production of its new flagship PX3 Platinum simulator manufactured by eCMMS, a top-to-bottom refinement of the training system that has revolutionized the way hitters train at the highest levels of competitive sports.

Rededicating its pledge to deliver the most user-friendly experience possible for its customers, ProBatter has also expanded its partnership with Vin D'Agostino of D'Agostino Industries Group to oversee product development and enhance engineering support, providing ease-of-care maintenance for its entire product line. Among his other significant accomplishments, Vin is an adjunct professor at Santa Clara University.

ProBatter has also partnered with Ardent Inc. of Greenville, NC, to expand its international sales network further, and Roman Media Group, LLC of Morris Plains, NJ, to oversee marketing via social media and internet channels. It has also re-engaged MediaVista Public Relations to handle media outreach and company communications for ProBatter and its customers.

V. Incorporating Video Pitching Simulators into Your Training Routine

A. Introduction

ProBatter understands that purchasing a ProBatter video pitching simulator for baseball, softball, or cricket is a significant expense for most customers. Reducing product costs has always been a priority in developing subsequent product generations. We have tried and will continue to work to come up with programs that make our units affordable through leasing, on-screen advertising, and sponsorship.

MAJOR LEAGUE BASEBALL

However, the value that ProBatter video simulators bring is that they improve the performance of their users. At various levels of these sports, particularly at the upper levels, player development is the ultimate goal. Increasing player performance can be a million-dollar problem at the Major League level.

ProBatter simulators help solve this million-dollar problem with an investment of less than $30,000. It should be appreciated that ProBatter's current price is less than a third of the price of the first simulator that it introduced almost 25 years ago and less than about twenty percent of the price of its only real competitor.

To maximize the value of this investment and get the most out of its features, ProBatter recommends that its users integrate their ProBatter units into the training routine. While the video features of ProBatter units almost make them live video games and, honestly, fun to use, they are a serious training tool for hitters of all ages. We continue to marvel at users who only use the simulator to throw the same pitch to the same location at the same speed, i.e., grooving pitch after pitch. While that might be fine for some users, it doesn't

take advantage of the true value of the simulators—facing different pitchers from both sides of the rubber throwing as many as eight different pitches at speeds between 35 and 100MPH to multiple locations inside and outside the strike zone—just like a real pitcher will pitch in a game.

The ProBatter simulators can also be used to train catchers in proper receiving and framing techniques and, importantly, to learn to block pitches in the dirt without having a coach bounce ball after ball at the catcher. It can mix up strikes vs. bouncing balls while keeping the catchers on their toes...literally.

B. Learning to Use the ProBatter® PX3 Simulator

The ProBatter Baseball Video Pitching Simulator is ideal for any level of baseball expertise. From Little Leaguers to Major Leaguers, the ProBatter Baseball Video Pitching Simulator can challenge players with a wide range of athletic abilities due to the many adjustable features that make the ProBatter pitching simulator a valuable tool in athletic training today. Together with its ease of use, the ProBatter Video Pitching Simulator provides a state-of-the-art batting experience that everyone can enjoy.

The ProBatter pitching simulator includes a video component that permits a batter to see a life-size image of an actual pitcher winding up and delivering a pitch thrown through a hole in the video projector screen by a computer-controlled pitch head. The user can select an age-appropriate, right-handed, or left-handed pitcher throwing from either a full windup or stretch position. The user can then program the simulator to interchangeably throw any pitch (fastball, sinker, cutter, splitter, curve, slider, changeup, etc.) that a real pitcher can throw at speeds up

RHP Pro Pitcher

to 100 MPH. Pitch speeds can be varied in increments of 2 mph, and pitches can be thrown to predetermined locations inside and outside the strike zone. The touchscreen mounted in the Operator Control Console or kiosk allows the user to fine-tune locations to provide ultimate pitching accuracy. The

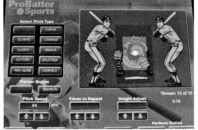

Touchscreen Controller for Baseball Unit

simulator can also adjust pitch location to suit both left and right-handed batting positions.

The ProBatter Baseball Video Pitching Simulator offers the following features:

- "Live" pitcher simulation. A combination of life-size images shows actual pitchers throwing realistic pitches, all integrated through computer controls. The ball is delivered through the screen in synchronization with the video image.

- Deliver any pitch at any speed. Pitches include the fastball, sinker, cutter, splitter, curve, slider, changeups, and slurves from right-handed and left-handed pitchers in 2 MPH increments to multiple locations inside and outside the strike zone.

- Accuracy. Pitches are delivered to the desired location with a typical repeatability of 5 inches.

- Range of pitcher options. Users can choose from a collection of on-screen, age-appropriate pitchers (from Little League to professional) who are either left or right-handed and deliver pitches from a full windup or stretch position.

- Range of batter options. Adjustable pitch height for batters, as well as skill level. Batters can hit from either side of the plate to suit left- and right-handed players.

- Manual and automatic modes. Pitch sequencing can be established on either a pitch-by-pitch basis using the Touchscreen on the Operator Control Console to set pitch type, speed, and location or by running one of the preprogrammed automatic sequences of pitches. Custom sequences are available on request.

ProBatter provides its customers with a detailed user manual for every unit, and the customer is encouraged to read the manual and become familiar with the various components. That will ensure that the customer performs the necessary maintenance steps, typical for every complex piece of an electromechanical machine.

C. Features of the ProBatter PX3 Simulator

The Video Screen

The Video Screen displays the life-size image of a pitcher winding up and delivering a pitch, which is actually thrown through the screen towards the batter.

Life Size Video Screen Display

Video Projector and Operator Control Unit

The video images are projected onto the screen by a digital projector that can be mounted using one of the two methods described in the manual. The Projector is connected to a power source and the Computer Cabinet.

Changes to the settings of the Video Projector are made with the remote-control device stored near the Control Cabinet. Initial settings are optimized at installation; however, installation conditions may change with time. Various digital projectors can be used with the ProBatter® Baseball Video Pitching Simulator. Consult the Projector manufacturer's instruction manual provided with your simulator for adjustment options.

Kiosk Mounted Touchscreen

The Operator Control Kiosk is located near home plate and is used by the batter or coach to select and activate pitches. Commands are entered through a Touchscreen Controller. The Operator

Control Console must be located where the operator and console will be protected from hit balls and swinging, flying, or broken bats.

Touchscreen Controller

A touchscreen controller is mounted in the Control Kiosk and is the "brains" of the PX3. It was designed for ease of use by ProBatter's customers and is the control interface for the unit. Using the Touchscreen controller, the user can choose such functions as the age level of the batter, types of pitches to throw at what speed and location, and whether the simulator should pitch in a manual mode where the pitch type is selected by the user on a pitch-by-pitch basis, a repeat mode where the same pitch is repeated over and over again to the same location and same Speed, or a randomized array of different pitches—like a pitcher throws in an actual game!

The touchscreen controller is the heart and soul of the PX3 simulator and is exceptionally user-friendly. That said, the customer needs to fully understand the touchscreen's operation to maximize the simulator's benefits.

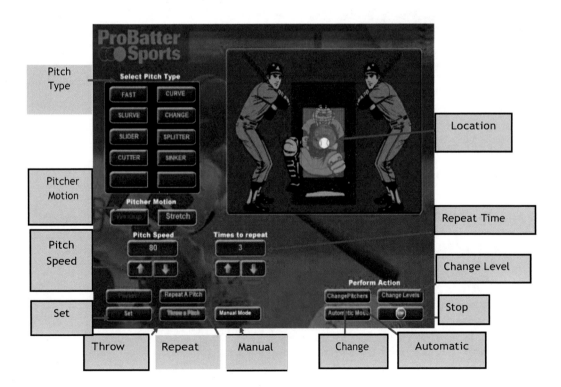

Pitch Head

The pitch head is the main working component of the ProBatter simulator. It includes three independently-controlled, rotating pitching wheels mounted on a support frame adapted to pivot in both a horizontal and vertical direction. Powerful DC drive motors power the wheels. An injector mechanism feeds balls into an area between the wheels called the "NIP," located between the grip points of the three rotating pitching wheels. The pitch head is lo-

3-wheel Pitch head

cated directly behind the video screen and is adapted to propel balls to the hitter through a hole in the screen.

Ball Feeder and Injector

Optional Barrel Ball Feeder

A ball Injector is positioned adjacent to the pitch head and is adapted to propel balls into the Nip between the rotating wheels to be propelled to the hitter.

An optional 225-ball barrel ball feeder is positioned downstream from the injector and is adapted to deliver balls to the injector for insertion into the pitch head. A ball sensor detects when a ball is in the "ready" position, determines if the buffer is full, and sends a signal to the control system to stop the Ball Feeder operation.

D. Profile Your Pitches to Make Them Age/Level Appropriate

A. Professional (18+)

1. Fastballs 85-100 MPH

2. Cutter for both lefty and righty (85-95)

3. O/H Curve (backing slightly off to (72-86)

4. Slider (80-90)

5. Changeup (74-84)

6. Screwball (80-90)

7. Sinker (80-90)

B. College Market (18+ and Over the Hill Gang)

1. Fastball (80-95)

2. Cutter for both lefty and righty (80-90)

3. O/H Curve (2/3 of what we currently have) (70-82)

4. Slider (75-85)

5. Changeup (70-80)

6. Screwball (75-85)

7. Sinker (75-85)

C. High School Market (16-18)

1. Fastball (75-90)

2. Cutter for both lefty and righty (75-85)

3. O/H Curve (1/2 of what we currently have) (65-75)

4. Slider (70-80)*

5. Changeup (65-75)

6. Sinker (70-85)*

D. Junior Babe Ruth (13-15)

1. Fastball (65-80)

2. Cutter for both lefty and righty (65-80)

3. O/H Curve (1/4 of what we currently have) (60-70)

4. Slider (60-75)*

5. Changeup (60-70)

6. Sinker (65-75)*

E. Little League (Majors) (11-12)

      1. Fastball (55-75)

      2. Cutter for both lefty and righty (55-75)

      3. O/H Curve (slight downward break (50-60)

      4. Changeup (50-60)

F. Little League (Minors) (9-10)

      1. Fastball (50-60)

      2. Changeup (40-55)

G. Little League (Cap League) (<9)

      1. Fastball (40-50)

E.   Uses for PX3 Video Pitching Simulator

Batting Practice Between Games

Customers regularly schedule sessions for their teams with the ProBatter simulators between games to prepare for the next game. The units can be set up to repeatedly throw pitches from either side of the plate that a hitter has had trouble with in a game.

Alternatively, the units can be preprogrammed to throw random selections of pitches that the hitter may expect to face in a game at the same speeds and locations and with varied pitch profiles to get them ready for the game.

Teach Situational Hitting

Using the manual selection mode, the coach can alert the hitter to a particular situation in a game with pitch count and inning, e.g., runner on second base, hit to the right side of the infield or runner on third base, try to get a flyball to the outfield, and have the hitter try to hit as instructed by the coach.

Bunting Practice

While bunting may, at some levels, be a lost art, at lower levels in the sport, it is still alive and well and is still an essential skill for young players to develop. The ProBatter simulator is a perfect training tool to teach hitters the old-fashioned art of bunting, almost like a basketball coach who concludes every practice with a free throw drill.

Pitch & Strike Zone Recognition

Many coaches rely on the ProBatter simulator for hitters to learn pitch recognition. They will have their hitter stand in the batter's box and watch pitch after pitch to try to understand the type of pitch being thrown by the release point of the pitch off the pitcher's hand and the spin of the seams on the ball. The beauty of the ProBatter system is that the ball comes through a hole in the screen. Since most curve balls rise above the release point vs. fastballs, which tend to be on the same line or below the release point, it is an easy and very effective way to teach pitch recognition.

It is also a great way to teach hitters the strike zone. Coaches have the hitter stand in the cage and watch pitch after pitch, telling the coach whether it's a ball or strike. When we first introduced the simulator at the MLB Winter Meetings in 1999, several MLB managers thought having hitters stand in and face a variety of pitches was a great way of teaching the strike zone to young hitters.

Warm Up Pinch Hitters

There may be no better way to prepare a hitter for a pinch-hitting appearance than ducking into the tunnel or gym and facing pitches of the type the pitcher delivers in a game. Far too many pinch hitters enter the game cold, explaining why the average batting average for pinch hitters is as low as it is.

Saving Coaches and Pitcher's Arms

Batting practice is a necessary part of baseball practice sessions. Far too many coaches, particularly at the lower levels of the sports, are either unwilling or incapable of throwing batting practice to give their hitters meaningful pitches, i.e., the type of pitches they will receive in the game. ProBatter simulators will do just that.

Training Catchers

Catching pitches from the ProBatter is an excellent training tool for catchers to improve their framing and receiving skills. Similarly, it is an excellent tool for training catchers in blocking pitches in the dirt without wearing out a coach's arm.

Development of Training Routine for ProBatter

A. 15 Minute Routine

B. 30 Minute Routine

C. 45 Minute Routine

D. 60 Minute Routine

Perfect for Hitting Leagues—Adds Competition to Batting Practice

Combine the ProBatter simulator with a Hittrax or Rapsodo unit, and you have the perfect "smart cage" to measure the results of a batting practice session. Unlike other pitching machines that combine with these ball tracking systems, the pitches they will face are on a level equal to the pitches they will see in a real game, not something like their grandmother would throw. In other words, it's a real competition.

ABOVE EVERYTHING ELSE---IT ADDS FUN AND EXCITEMENT TO OTHERWISE BORING BATTING PRACTICE!

VI. Converting Conventional Pitching Machines to Video Machines

A. Introduction

ProBatter understands that non-video pitching machines have been used successfully for the past half-century, and, without doubt, virtually every baseball, softball, or cricket player has trained, at one point or another, on such machines. They are the industry's staple and have helped hitters and batters of all ages and all types.

There are a wide variety of such machines, including:

- Manually Operated Pitching Machines

- Battery-Powered Pitching Machines

- Electric Motor-Powered Pitching Machines: Non-portable

- Electric Motor-Powered Pitching Machines: Portable

- One-wheel Pitching Machines

- Two-wheel Pitching Machines

- Three-wheel Pitching Machines

Row of ProBatter Simulators

"Arm" machines, such as the venerable Iron Mike machine, are the staple of pitching machines used in many batting cages and training centers.

While the two-wheeled pitching machines marketed by Jugs and Atec were the dominant force in such machines for decades, they have been replaced by three-wheel machines sold by Jugs, Atec, Spinball, and Hack Attack, all of whom followed the lead of ProBatter Sports after they introduced the first ProBatter Professional in 1999. Three-wheel machines offer significant benefits over two-wheel machines because they can create lateral movement of the pitches without having to adjust the position of the machine. Today, virtually every pitching machine company offers a three-wheel machine in one form or another, and, generally speaking, these machines are very good at what they accomplish—providing excellent batting practice for hitters and batters of all ages.

While ProBatter would urge serious customers to consider and purchase its top-of-the-line PX3 video pitching simulator, it recognizes that most people have a significant investment in their existing conventional pitching machines and would seek less expensive alternatives.

With that in mind, ProBatter developed and has sold hundreds of its Pro-Batter PB II video conversion kits over the past two decades for most conventional pitching machines, including Master Pitch's Iron Mike machine and Sports Attack's Hack Attack machines. ProBatter is currently working on converting other conventional pitching machines, including the ABC machines.

The advantage of these conversion kits is that they represent a relatively low-cost way to enter the video pitching machine market because, in many instances, the customer already has the conventional machine.

The PBII Conversion Kit provides the equipment and electronics required to convert that conventional pitching machine into a video simulator at a small fraction of the cost of purchasing our top-of-the-line PX3 simulator.

Specifically, the conversion kit provides:

- a frame for attachment to the conventional pitching machine;

- a projection screen adapted to be mounted on the frame;

- a video projector for projecting the video image of actual pitchers onto the projection screen; and

- a computer controller for storing multiple images of pitchers and synchronizing those images with the release of pitches from the pitching machine.

B. The Cost

Purchase Options

A PB II Conversion kit for an Iron Mike machine costs **$7995**, while the PB II conversion kit for a Hack Attack machine costs **$15,450**. Substantial discounts are available for multiple unit purchases, e.g., a 5% savings per each additional conversion kit purchased. Talk with our sales department about discounts on three or more conversion kits.

For customers who don't already own an Iron Mike or Hack Attack unit, ProBatter offers complete packages with both the pitching machine and the conversion kit at similarly low prices, e.g., **$12,450** for a complete Iron Mike unit or **$29,999** for a complete e-Hack Attack unit (lower costs for the Junior Hack Attack or the regular Hack Attack units).

Leasing Options

Leasing options for the ProBatter PB II Conversion Kits (and complete units) are available to qualified customers with established good credit.

For example, a 48-month lease-to-buy option for a PB II Iron Mike Conversion kit would be approximately **$195 per Month** with a residual value of $500. Similarly, a 48-month lease-to-buy option for a PB II Hack Attack Conversion kit would be approximately **$395 per Month**.[1]

C.   Making Money with PB II Units

In addition to the apparent training advantages the PB II Conversion kit offers, these kits can be money-makers for their owners, whether they are commercial facilities or teams, for the following reasons.

It should be appreciated that customers not only like the video conversions of conventional pitching machines but are willing to pay a premium to use them. As such, commercial batting cages shouldn't be reluctant to charge a premium for video cages, and they will find that their customers will readily pay for them because of the increased value and experience. For example, if a cage regularly charged $3 for a round of 20 pitches, increasing that price to either $3.50 or decreasing the number of pitches per round to 15 would easily

---

[1] Leasing charges are based on a 10% interest rate over 48 months with a residual value of approximately 10%. Charges will vary depending upon the credit history of the borrower.

cover the lease costs of a PB II conversion kit. Similarly, adding a $10 surcharge to its hourly rates would yield a significant profit over its current costs because of the increased use of that cage.

Both commercial batting cages and teams can avail themselves of the possibility of on-screen advertising and sponsorship opportunities, which will quickly cover the monthly lease charges.

D. Applications of ProBatter PB II Video Units

ProBatter PB II Video Conversion Kits are helpful for a variety of applications.

Commercial Batting Cages

Most of the PB II units ProBatter sells are used in commercial batting cages, typically in the token or card-operated sections, to convert their existing Iron Mike machines.

While some operators are happy to install a single PB II unit in a bank of cages to "try it out," most quickly find that their customers gravitate to the video cage at the exclusion of the others, even though the price is slightly higher. As such, they will

Facility with Multiple PB II units

eventually install multiple PB II units for ALL of their cages. Since multiple unit discounts are available, that is a very cost-effective way for operators to justify their investment.

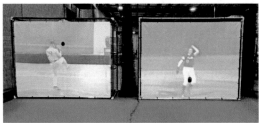

Side by Side Baseball & Softball Machines

The PB II units are available for baseball, softball, and cricket. As such, it's not uncommon for operators to have two different sports in adjacent cages to ensure they appeal to players of both sports. For example, adjacent baseball and softball cages are typical and generally popular with customers.

PB II Video Units are perfect for hitting leagues sponsored by the commercial cage or training center. Combine the PB II unit with a Hittrax or

Rapsodo unit, and you have the perfect Smart Cage where coaches can measure the results of a batting practice session. In other words, it's a real competition.

Team and Player Applications

Hitter Facing a PB II

While the PB II units were initially designed for commercial batting cages, ProBatter has found they have had equal application with individual players, colleges, high schools, and teams who own conventional pitching machines and want to convert them to video simulators. These customers have quickly learned and appreciated the competitive advantages of using video simulators over the "roll down the tube" conventional pitching machines, as they have found that they have better prepared them for competition in game-like conditions. Again, PB II units are available for baseball, softball, and even cricket.

Iron Mike PB II on Wheels

One of the issues facing some schools and facilities is that they may be sharing their cages with other sports. As such, it may be necessary to have a "mobile" pitching machine that can be moved into and out of the cage before and after batting practice. ProBatter has a solution to that problem—placing the Iron Mike machine and the video frame on casters or wheels that can be rolled into and out of the batting cage.

VII. Video Pitching Simulators—The Ultimate Entertainment Product

While the ProBatter PX3 Video Simulator is the "Ultimate Training Product," it is also the "Ultimate Entertainment Product" for one primary reason—it is fun to use and always draws a crowd. While the multi-pitch PX3 units are the gold standard for training, the PB II video conversion kits are more commonly used for entertainment and promotions, primarily because of their significantly lower cost.

Promotional Activities

PB II Video Conversion kits are regularly used as "attractions" to help promote various products since they tend to be crowd-gatherers. We live in a world where experiential products have proven to be highly effective in generating interest and crowds. A video batting cage is the ultimate experiential product.

PB II Batting Cage at MLB All Star Game

Leading consumer products companies such as Nike, Right Guard, AT&T, Adidas, and others have used PB II video units to attract attention for various events and openings. Their presence is always sure to attract people and attention to the products that are being promoted.

Video Batting Cage Trade Show Booth

These units are also commonly used at trade shows to attract attention to an exhibitor's underlying products or services. For many years, a leading sporting goods company has wanted to select a trade show booth across the aisle from ProBatter because they recognized that the ProBatter batting cage would attract attention and there would be a line of people waiting to use it.

While waiting in line, they couldn't help but notice the products the sporting goods company displayed.

Similarly, because they are fun to use and watch, they have been successfully used as attractions at various sporting and corporate events, including All-Star Games, corporate parties and outings, fan affairs at ballparks, etc.

ProBatter at Superbowl Party

Fan Attraction Units

MLB and Minor League teams are always looking for a way to attract

ProBatter at Coors Field in Denver

ProBatter at Turner Field in Atlanta

more fans and engage their fans before and during games, and the PB II video batting cages are the best way to accomplish that goal. Because the unit will display a range of available pitchers, such cages are a top-rated attraction for the team and its fans. They can be installed in the stadium concourses or out-

Outdoor Installation at Minor League Stadium

side the stadium using an inflatable batting cage.

Providing a batting cage at a baseball stadium for use by the fans is the "ultimate" experiential experience. Clubs have developed videos of their pitchers for display on the screen. Imagine the excitement of a ten-year-old being able to hit against a video of the starting pitcher for the actual game. That is a dream that every youngster will remember for the rest of their life.

Revenue Generators

One of the distinct advantages of a video pitching machine is the ability to display a sponsor's or advertiser's message either adjacent to the video image of the pitcher or on the video screen between rounds. This can be done at both batting cages and stadiums for fan use.

Sponsor Display Adjacent Screen

Most batting cages include a "Pro Shop" where customers can purchase various products like bats, gloves, balls, and apparel. Imagine allowing the manufacturer or supplier of those products to advertise or promote them on the same video screen the customer views when hitting against the ProBatter video simulator. It is a great way to promote these products, and the revenue generated from this advertising or sponsorship helps underwrite the cost of the units. ProBatter units have state-of-the-art audio and video capabilities, allowing sponsors or advertisers to play videos or other ads.

A sponsor or advertiser message can even be displayed on the outfield wall behind the pitcher on the pitcher video.

The ability to include these messages makes using the ProBatter video pitching simulator a revenue generator. Batting cages and clubs are always looking for the ability to generate revenue. Advertisers or sponsors will gladly help underwrite the cost of such units because they can be assured that thousands will see their message before and during a batting cage round or a game. It's a win-win for the operator, its customers, the team, and its fans.

Portable "Tunnels to Go" Units

ProBatter's "Tunnels to Go" product brings a ProBatter video simulator, complete with an inflatable batting tunnel, to the parking lot or sidewalk near you.

Tunnels to Go at a Stadium

It's relatively easy to mount an Iron Mike machine and a PB II video conversion kit into a trailer with an inflatable batting cage to create the "Tunnels to Go" product. These units are excellent for going on the road and bringing the units to the users. They are particularly effective for fan use at stadiums, promotional opportunities at various facilities, etc.

ProBatter has derived enormous publicity with its Tunnels to Go units, which have appeared on such television shows as Fox & Friends with Geraldo Rivera, CBS Morning News, ESPN, and dozens of local and regional television stations. The Tunnels to Go unit was used at the MLB All-Star game in San Francisco.

Fox & Friends Geraldo Hitting

VIII.   A True Smart Cage

A. Introduction

Since time in memoriam, players have gone into batting cages to hit against pitching and bowling machines to perfect their craft. However, the problem with batting cages is that while they can help hitters practice their craft, it is difficult, if not impossible, to determine their success rate and, perhaps, more importantly, record the event to learn from their mistakes.

Most batting cages employ conventional pitching machines, meaning hitters will repeatedly face the same pitch delivered at the same speed to the exact location. As discussed previously, such machines do not prepare the players to face a pitcher in an actual game since pitchers don't pitch that way.

Similarly, facing a conventional pitching machine without a video component does little, if anything, to allow a hitter or batter to be able to time a pitcher or bowler's windup or approach. Instead, they are forced to watch a ball roll down a chute or a light to appear, signaling that the pitch is about to be released. Again, that's not the real world and unquestionably violates ProBatter's core precept of the "**Practice Like You Play**" concept.

Enter the ProBatter PX3 video pitching simulator, which allows a hitter or batter to face various pitches, all delivered at different speeds to different locations. The PX3 places hitters in a game-like environment to face the type of pitchers and the "stuff" they will face in a real game.

The Smart Cage

The Smart Cage employs a programmable **ProBatter® PX3** video simu-

lator as its standard pitching machine because of its ability to consistently and accurately throw any pitch that a pitcher can throw and incorporates a video front to provide a game-like experience for the hitter and the ability to time the pitch.

ProBatter PX3 in Action

The ProBatter system can throw more than eight pitches from left-handed and right-handed pitchers and bowlers at speeds between 65 and 100 MPH. It has been the accepted industry leader for video pitching simulators since 2000 and is used at all baseball, softball, and cricket levels.

Hittrax Display for Baseball

How does the Smart Cage determine the success rate of a hitter? Simple. It includes the Hittrax® ball tracking system that tracks the path and velocity of the batted ball and provides analytical data concerning the hitter's performance, e.g., the hitter's bat speed, the distance the batted ball would travel in a non-cage environment, the angle of the hit relative to the pitch, etc. Such data is displayed digitally and graphically on the ProBatter video screen to provide quantitative data relative to the at-bat.

The Hittrax system provides the following analytics:

- Exit Velocity

- Launch Angle

- Distance

- Point of Impact

- Play Outcome

- Strike Zone Analysis

- High-Speed Video w/ integrated metrics

The third component of the Smart Cage is a recording component so that the hitter or their coach can review the session at their leisure to analyze their session and determine what the hitter or batter could do to improve their performance.

Video Record of At Bat

Enter a video recording system such as Right View Pro™, which makes a permanent video recording of the at-bat for each hitter and allows the results to be streamed to a remote coach or scout to evaluate the hitter's performance. The coach or scout can visually observe how the prospect handled a particular pitch or his swing and mechanics. The coach or scout can mark up or "telestrate" the video to show the prospect what he did and how he can improve his performance.

The Smart Cage Plus

The "Smart Cage Plus" goes one step further by analyzing and evaluating pitchers by incorporating the ProBatter's **Strike Out Pro**™ pitcher trainer, which tests and evaluates a pitcher's effectiveness in pitching simulated

Strike Out Pro Unit

games. Specifically, it identifies and displays on a projection screen or pitcher target "hot" zones for different hitters and tests the pitcher's ability to hit these hot zones while measuring the speed of the individual pitch. Strike Out Pro will allow the pitcher to pitch to various

left-handed and right-hand batters.

The Smart Cage Plus would similarly be married with the Hittrax pitching tracking system, which further provides the following analytics:

- Pitch Location

- Late Break Measurement

- % Strikes

- Performance by Pitch Type

- Opposing Batting Stats

- High-Speed Video w/ integrated metrics

A video recording system like Right View Pro would be included to complete the Smart Cage Plus for Pitchers.

B.   Applications

Smart Cages are an excellent way to evaluate the performance of both hitters and pitchers for scouting purposes and to stage competitions between players, teams, and event facilities. Because of the consistency offered by the ProBatter PX3 pitching system, it establishes a "level" playing field in which every player or team is forced to compete. They allow hitters or pitchers of all ages to measure their performances against a standard pitch sequence to determine how they will perform at various levels of the sport.

Measuring a hitter's performance against a conventional pitching machine does not translate to real-world performance expectations since actual game pitchers do not pitch the way conventional pitching machines pitch.

Competitions

Using Smart Cages for internal competitions or competitions between different facilities is an excellent way for players and teams to compete against a common standard. Every participant would face the same sequence of pitches thrown by the ProBatter PX3 video simulator, and their performance would be measured by the Hittrax system and recorded by the Right View Pro video recording system.

As such, the Smart Cages are perfect for conducting hitting leagues at various batting cages since the participants will all be measured against a standard sequence of pitches, i.e., throwing the same pitches at the same speeds in identical sequences. The sequences of pitches and the individual pitches constituting the sequence will be age and level-appropriate. For example, older players will each face faster pitches with more pitch movement than younger players at the Middle or High School levels.

Setting up a network of Smart Cages around an area or, for that matter, around the country will allow batting cages and training centers to compete against each other in hitting leagues since the participants will all face the same level and type of pitches at each location. The Hittrax and Right View Pro systems will measure and record performance to ensure accurate results are recorded.

Such a competition could generate sufficient interest and participation to produce a televised (and sponsored) competition, potentially resulting in a "World Series" of batting cage competitions.

Scouting

Scouting showcases have existed for the last couple of decades, where prospects are brought to a central location where scouts from professional and college teams can watch them play in games against elite competition. Perfect

Game USA is the unquestioned showcase leader, running scores of showcases, tournaments, and leagues where scouts can see players. They also offer player reports and video services. While these showcases are an excellent way to evaluate a player's abilities and performance, one downside is that they force a player to travel to distant locations, and, perhaps more significantly, the level of competition may vary, which may skew the results.

Using a Smart Cage to evaluate performance is a more consistent way to evaluate a player's abilities and projected performance. Hitting at a showcase tournament against a pitcher projected to play college, professional baseball, or softball will be helpful, but that is not always the case. Frequently, the hitters will find themselves facing pitchers who will never move to that next level.

With the Smart Cage, a scout can evaluate hitters against a standard sequence of the type of pitches that the hitters will face at their current level and, perhaps more importantly, at the next level. Evaluating a hitter facing an 85 MPH fastball does not always equate to their performance against a pitcher throwing a 95 MPH fastball that they may face at the next level. Putting that same hitter in a Smart Cage against a pitcher throwing that speed and measuring and recording the player's performance will give the scout or recruiter a better picture of what that player can do at the next level.

Providing the Hittrax analytics and the video recording further allows the scout or recruiter to fully evaluate the hitter's performance and determine what can be done to improve performance.

The advantage of the video recording system in a Smart Cage is that it allows a remote evaluation of the player—the scout or recruiter doesn't need to travel far and wide to scout or evaluate the player. They need only to get a recording of the player's performance in the Smart Cage to determine whether the player is of interest.

It should be appreciated that the Smart Cage is not a replacement for evaluating a player's performance in a real game. That can never be replaced. What it can do, however, is help the scout or recruiter prioritize who they should observe and where they should travel, thereby lessening the travel burdens of the scout or recruiter.

Sponsorship Opportunities

The Smart Cage offers an excellent opportunity for a facility to attract sponsors interested in an established brand. Possible sponsors for such Smart Cages are equipment providers such as Wilson, Nike, or Rawlings; service providers such as IMG or other sports agencies; or established players or managers.

Revenue Opportunities

Smart Cages offer facilities an excellent source of revenue possibilities, including:

- A Facility Rental Fee paid by the batting cage or training center where the units are housed;

- A Prospect Fee paid by the prospects using the services;

- A Scouting Subscription Fee paid by the professional and college teams to access the data; and

- A sponsorship fee paid by the naming sponsorship.

IX. The Cost of Video Pitching Simulators

A. Purchase Prices

Video Pitching Simulators

- ProBatter PX3 Video Baseball Pitching Simulator ($27,495)
- ProBatter PX3 Video Softball Pitching Simulator ($27,495)
- ProBatter PX3 Video Cricket Bowling Simulator ($27,495)
- ProBatter PX3 "Combo" Video Simulators ($49,995)
- ProBatter II Video Conversion Kits for Iron Mike Pitching Machines ($7,995)
- ProBatter II Video Version of Iron Mike Pitching Machines ($15,450)

Available Options

- 225 ball barrel feeder ($2,500)
- 12-ball sleeve feeder ($500)
- Hittrax Integration (Call for pricing)
- Updated Video Pitcher Package (Call for pricing)
- Upgraded 5000 lumen projector (+$500)

Other Training Products

- Smart Cage Batting Cages ($49,500)
- Smart Cage Plus Cage ($75,000)
- Challenger Non-Video Pitching Machine ($15,995)
- Strike Out Pro Pitcher Trainer ($14,995)

B. Leasing Options

ProBatter has a relationship with several leasing companies that offer low-cost lease options to credit-worthy customers. For example, monthly costs for a 5-year lease for each of these products with 5% down and a $1 buyout at 12% interest can be as low as:

- ProBatter PX3 Video Baseball Pitching Simulator ($565/mo.)
- ProBatter PX3 Video Softball Pitching Simulator ($565/mo.)
- ProBatter PX3 Video Cricket Bowling Simulator ($565/mo.)
- ProBatter PX3 "Combo" Video Simulators ($1,030/mo.)
- ProBatter II Video Conversion Kits for Iron Mike Pitching Machines ($165/mo.)
- ProBatter II Video Version of Iron Mike Pitching Machines ($325/mo.)
- Smart Cage (CALL)
- Smart Cage Plus (CALL)

X.   Affording & Making Money with ProBatter Units

ProBatter recognizes and understands that purchasing a video pitching simulator like the PX3 or even converting an existing conventional pitching machine to a video pitching machine can be expensive and, to some people, daunting. The purpose of this section is to explain why such a purchase should not impede moving your facility into the 21st century. More importantly, by "adjusting" your typical use charges, you can frequently cover the cost of the ProBatter video pitching machines and, perhaps even more importantly, **increase your profitability**.

For starters, the ProBatter video simulators are attention grabbers. Customers want to come and use these pieces of equipment, so for that reason alone, your revenues should increase. Customers are always drawn to the "newest and greatest," and that's precisely what the ProBatter units are when compared to conventional pitching machines of the prior generation.

Adjusted Pricing

That said, while adding these simulators will undoubtedly raise your overall revenue numbers if you want to similarly increase your profitability (because your expense side will increase), you should also consider adjusting your pricing for using ProBatter simulators over conventional pitching machines.

For example, suppose you were charging $3 for a round of 20 pitches against a pitching machine that costs $5,000. In that case, customers will understand and expect they will have to pay a higher charge for the same number of pitches for a PB II video simulator that may have a combined cost of $15,000.

There are several ways of achieving this. For example, a facility might:

- Increase the cost for a 20-pitch round from $3 to $5: or

- Maintain the current pricing but decrease the number of pitches in the round from 20 to 12 or 15;

- A combination of the two, e.g., raising the price from $3 to $5 per round while decreasing the number of pitches to 12 or 15.

The ProBatter PX3 multi-pitch video simulators are frequently used in tunnels rather than cages, and facilities typically rent out time for the tunnels on a half-hour or hourly basis for team and individual training sessions. Our more successful customers have found that they can easily cover the increased cost of the PX3 by adding the following "surcharge" to their existing fees:

- For Team and individual rentals by the hour or half-hour, adding a surcharge of $15-20/hour;
- Where the PX3 is used for lessons, etc., adding a surcharge of $10/hour);
- Where the PX3 is used for hitting leagues, adding a surcharge of $15-20/team;
- Where the PX3 is used for hitting leagues in conjunction with a HitTrax tracking system, adding a surcharge of $25/team.

A number of our more successful customers have created a PX3 Club for their dedicated players/teams, where they pre-sell time for the use of the simulators. Pre-selling time is an excellent way to accelerate cash flow and protect the facility from the vagaries of daily use.

Leasing Options

Looking at the purchase price of a ProBatter PX3 simulator—even a PB II Conversion Kit can be imposing. ProBatter understands this and has negotiated with a leasing company to provide an attractive leasing alternative so the facility doesn't have to face the initial purchase payment. As noted above, leases are available to credit-worthy customers who can stretch their payments out for four or even five years and reduce monthly costs to under $600 per Month for a PX3 video simulator; about $1000 per Month for a PX3 combo simulator; about $325 a month for a ProBatter II Video Version of Iron Mike Pitching Machines; and as low as $165 a month for a video conversion kit for your current conventional pitching machine.

On-Screen Advertising/Sponsorship

As noted earlier, ProBatter units are ideal for displaying a sponsor's or advertiser's message. They can be aired between rounds, on the outfield wall for each pitcher, on the side of cages, etc. For a facility that has a Pro Shop, they are an excellent way to advertise or promote certain products that are being sold in that shop.

ProBatter will assist its customers in developing such an advertising or sponsorship program and work with the customer in creating an appropriate ad or message to be displayed.

The financial results of advertising or sponsorship displays can be enormous. For example, suppose the facility generates at least $600/month in advertising or sponsorship revenue. In that case, it will cover the lease costs of four PB II Conversion kits or two PB II Complete units with a pitching machine. Similarly, it would cover a significant portion of the cost of a PX3 simulator.

Financial Models

The following are sample financial models for a PB II Conversion kit and a PX3 video pitching simulator.

PROBATTER II IRON MIKE CONVERSION WORKSHEET

	No.	Surcharge	ProBatter II
ProBatter II Annual Lease Cost	1,980		
Annual Pitch Total	150,000		
Pitches/Round	20		
Price/Round Surcharge		$ 1	$ 7,500
Cage Rentals	240	$ 10	$ 2,400
Cage Revenues			$ 9,900
Hitting League Members	25	$ 10	$ 3,000
Club Membership	10	$ 50	$ 6,000
Lesson Surcharge	60	$ 5	$ 3,600
Annual Revenue			
Annual Revenue			$ 22,500.00
Advertising Revenue			$ -
Gross Annual Revenue			$ 22,500.00
Annual Expenses			
Annual Equipment Cost			$ 1,980.00
Equipment Maintenance			$ 500.00
Gross Annual Expenses			$ 2,480.00
Based on the data that you entered, your Net Annual Profit is:			
Net Annual Profit			$20,020.00

PROBATTER PX3 WORKSHEET

ProBatter PX3 cost	See prices at the right		$ -27,495
ProBatter I Mo. Lease Cost			$ 565
Mo. Maintenance Cost			$ 25
Utilization			
Daily Operating Hours			12
Days Per Month			30
Percent Utilization			50%
Hrs./Year Utilized			2160
Annual Revenue	No./Month	Surcharge	
Tunnel Rental Surcharge	15	$ 15	$ 2,700
Lesson Surcharge	36	$ 10	$ 4,320
Hitting League Members Surcharge	15	$ 15	$ 2,700
Club Membership	10	$ 125	$ 15,000
Sponsorship/Ad Revenue	2 sponsors/advertisers	$ 200/Month	$ 2,400
Gross Annual Revenue			$ 27,120
Annual Expenses			
Annual Lease Cost			$ 6,780
Annual Maintenance Cost			$ 300
Gross Annual Expenses			$ 7,080
Based on the data that you entered, your Net Annual Profit			
after installing a PX3 in your tunnel			
Net Annual Profit			$ 20,040

XI.   Getting Recruited—A Guide to Playing in College[2]

A. Introduction

If your (or your son's) goal is to play college baseball, get ready for what will likely be the most challenging process you will have gone through to date. Recruiting isn't for the faint of heart.

The Numbers

Why, you ask? Let's start with the figures below:

Estimated probability of competing in college baseball

High School Participants	NCAA Participants	Overall % HS to NCAA	% HS to NCAA Division I	% HS to NCAA Division II	% HS to NCAA Division III
482,740	36,011	7.3%	2.2%	2.2%	2.9%

While these numbers change slightly from year to year, the fact remains this is a very competitive process. If you break down these numbers further, it gets even more difficult. The total percentage of those moving on from high school to college is 7.3%, but it's half that number. Approximately half the recruited players are pitchers and the other half position players. So, one has a 3.65% chance of being recruited as a position player or a pitcher. Put another way, if you are a high school pitcher or position player, you have a 94.35% chance that you won't play baseball in college.

In addition, only Division 1 and Division 2 can offer baseball scholarships. Out of the 4.4% of players at these levels, half of these recruits will typically get baseball money. So, again, doing the math, you have a 2.2% chance of getting scholarship money for college baseball, which means 1.1% for pitchers and 1.1% for position players.

---

[2] Written by Wayne "Coach Mazz" Mazzoni has been a D1 college coach for more than 30 years and operates a consulting company in Fairfield County, CT coaching and counseling high school players on college scholarship opportunities. He is a regular guest on WFAN, the host of ProBatter's Podcast entitled "And That Is the Game," and the author of a number of books on the subject, including *Getting Recruited: The Definitive Guide to Playing College Sport*s which is available on Amazon and other books outlets. He can be reached at wayne@waynemazzoni.com.

The Recruiting Process

The recruiting process is very confusing, inexact, and overwhelming for players, parents, and, believe it or not, college coaches. So, to bring some structure to this process, athletes must go through three distinct stages from the start of the recruiting process until they commit to a school.

Three Stages

Step One:

The first step to making this process more manageable is for each player to narrow down the places where they would like to attend/get recruited. Unless you are one of the best players in your area, if you don't have a workable list of schools, you will be lost and overwhelmed with the recruiting process.

In creating this list, you should consider at least three factors to narrow the list of possible schools.

The first factor is academics. Based on the player's academic profile and interests, he should start to narrow the list of colleges that would be a fit. Almost every high school uses college search tools to help narrow a student's list of possible colleges from an academic standpoint. College Board scores are one such tool, while Naviance is a software product that provides students with college planning and career assessment tools.

The second factor is personal preference. There are many different college experiences, some better than others, but each different. By visiting as many schools as you can, players can determine factors such as setting (city, suburb, rural), enrollment size (huge, large, medium, small, tiny), location (close to home or far), and whatever else is essential to each person.

The best way to determine a student's personal preference is to visit schools in your current geographic area. See all the different types of schools. You don't need to do a formal tour at first-- see what feels comfortable and what doesn't. The more you see, the easier it will be to determine what you like and dislike. For example, do you want to be within 5 hours of home? Do you prefer small schools or larger ones with at least 10,000 (or more) students? Do you want to be in the city or a rural setting? Does the school have the major you're interested in pursuing? Quickly, a list of schools will start to emerge.

Using these two factors so far, academics and preferences, you should be able to get to a list of 50-100 schools that make sense. It could be fewer or more, but at least you have a list and some focus.

Then comes **the third factor: baseball talent**. The sooner you can get an idea of where you stack up as far as talent at the college level, the sooner your list can become more focused.

By doing the combination of the things I will suggest below, you should start to get an idea if you are a high-level Division 1, lower Division 1, high Division 2, lower Division 2, high Division 3, lower Division 3, or Division 4 (there is no Division 4!) player.

Watch college games either on television or, better yet, in person; ask your high school and travel coaches what they recommend; talk to your friends playing in college; get evaluated at recruiting camps or showcases; use some metrics to see where you stack up. By doing as many of these things as possible, you should get an idea of where you stand in terms of the college level.

So let's say, for example, you do your research, and it appears you are a high-level Division 3 player. So, you take your previous list of schools and start looking at who has baseball programs around your level of play. It could be as few as five schools or as many as forty, but you now have a structure that will help you as you get to the next step of the process.

The process I described is similar to a job search. When one looks for a job, they don't say they will do any work anywhere in the world. They narrow it down. I want to work in finance in Boston. I want to do marketing within an hour of where I live. I want to work at a law firm in Westchester County. The goals may vary, but there needs to be one.

In the recruiting world, the process can be overwhelming without a list and structure. This list can change based on many factors: deciding on a different major, realizing you don't want to go as far from home as you initially thought, your baseball talent may be better than you thought, making opportunities with higher level schools more realistic.

Step Two:

Once you have your list, it's time for step 2: Bridging the Gap.

For reasons mentioned at the start of this chapter, it is challenging for college coaches to sort through all the kids looking to play baseball at their school. Think of it this way. Let's take University X, a Division 1 school. This school likely has three to four coaches who handle the recruiting process. And let's say they will bring in 12 new players for each recruiting class--6 position players and 6 pitchers.

It is very likely that to settle on that class of 12, they may have had some interaction with 5,000 players. Plus, another 5,000 would have loved to have gotten their attention but didn't know how to make that happen.

Here is the point: you must do a combination of things to go from a complete "unknown" to a "known" commodity by the coaches at the schools on your list. Even then, it certainly won't guarantee that you get recruited by that school. Still, most of the 92.7% who don't play in college never got as far as getting evaluated and rejected from a school.

So what we are about to discuss will help you get in front of the schools on your list, and then your job is to be good enough to get them to recruit you. While talent always wins out, most students don't know how to bridge the gap of getting evaluated by the schools on their list. So what do you do? You do the following.

You should have a good video. The video can be practice footage (with metrics best, but without can work too) and highlights from games, provided that the video is close enough. You can put it on YouTube or Twitter and email it directly to coaches.

You should have trusted coaches call on your behalf. College coaches rely on trustworthy people to tell them about players to evaluate. When a job opens up, and thousands of resumes get sent in, they don't all get read, or all get an interview. Often, a resume gets pulled out of the pile through a connection or reference. It doesn't mean that person will get the job, but they moved ahead.

The same applies to references from a known coach. Perhaps your video gets watched, or the coach follows you online or comes to one of your games. This leads to the ultimate way to get recruited.

Be seen playing live. It sounds easy, but it's more complicated in reality. When you are playing your high school season, college coaches are also busy coaching their teams.

When you are playing in a summer tournament, there are hundreds of teams there, many playing at once, spread out over several fields. And this is one of many events going on.

This is why camps are so popular. While there are many types of camps, too many to list and describe here, my advice is to go to the college's camp. There are several benefits to these types of camps, e.g., they are the cheapest version of camps; you get to see the school and facilities; you get to be evaluated by the entire coaching staff; you often get to meet players on the team; and the coaches get to work you out in their preferred way. This allows you to start a connection and a relationship with the coaches.

If you do go to some of these prospect camps, be sure to follow up. If you can, try to find out what notes the coaches have taken on you, what they liked, what they thought needed work, and where you stand regarding their interest level.

Sometimes, larger camps make sense, meaning camps run by third-party businesses that hire college coaches to attend. There are benefits and drawbacks to some of these types of camps. The benefits are that you know the coaches will be there as they've been hired to attend. Unlike a typical summer game or tournament where you don't know which coaches will attend, and if they do, if it's the right school for you, many of the camps actually list the coaches who will be attending. Another benefit is that multiple schools can see you at one event.

Many of these events accurately record your metrics (time in the 60, home to first, pop times, throwing velocities, exit velocities, mound velocities, spin rates, etc. Plus, you will have a chance to do a practice-style workout and also compete in actual games.

The negative to some of these larger events is that the coaches being hired are often younger or assistant coaches who don't have as much recruiting influence as you think. In addition, these camps get many players, so it is easy to get overlooked.

Lastly, coaches often get hired for so many of these events, resulting in all the kids and players becoming blurred together, and they can get overwhelmed by the number of players they see.

Finally, sometimes coaches see players they like but figure, based on the other schools at these events, they won't have a shot competing for this player.

This is again why I like school camps directly. If you want to play at Bryant, you need to be seen by the Bryant coaches and staff. While there are several paths to this, being seen at one of their prospect camps is one of the quickest ways to find out if they are interested.

Recruiting is usually a combination of these three ways (video, recommendations, and live) that will be what gets someone evaluated. Perhaps you send an email with a video that the coach doesn't look at because he gets too many, but the call from your high school coach gets the college coach to locate and watch your video, and after watching it, he thinks you are good enough to watch during the high school or summer season.

Again, getting college coaches to evaluate you is what your goal should be in the recruiting process. If you have a list of twenty schools and twelve get to see you, and two or three really like you, you are well on your way to being recruited to play baseball in college.

If the coach doesn't start recruiting, you find out if it is based on his recruiting needs (doesn't need a catcher in your class), or doesn't think you are good enough, or maybe your academics aren't strong enough.

The more feedback you get, the more you adjust your list. If your list had 19 Division 1 schools and you hear from 10 that they don't think you are good enough, it's time to A) improve in whatever area you are deficient or B) redo your list of schools.

One final word in this section: Having been a college coach for 30 years, written three books on recruiting, spoken at over 500 high schools to players and parents on recruiting, and now running my own business guiding players on the process, I know that 99% of kids want to play Division 1.

I get it. Why not shoot for the highest level of baseball? However, many also think the lower levels are an easy fallback plan. So if Vanderbilt, LSU, and Duke don't offer, recruiting from one of the D3 schools should be easy.

The reality is since COVID and the transfer portal, Division 3, which was already strong, is now stronger than ever. **Getting recruited to a Division 3 school is very very hard.** How do I know this? I know this because 93% of high school players aren't good enough to play in college! The next level is for those who love it, work at it, and have elite talent. You have to be good, and then you have to have a recruiting plan.

Step Three:

The final step in the process happens when you get recruited from college coaches.

To explain what I mean, I typically use an example from the world of work. Let's say you have been out of work for six months. So you do all the things necessary to get a new job. You've sent resumes, applied for openings, networked, attended job fairs, etc. Then, all of a sudden, all your work pays off, and, over two weeks, you have six interviews for jobs you like.

Now imagine that on the following Monday, all six call to offer you a job. Awesome, right? But which one will you take?

I imagine you'd have many questions for the employer before you pick your new job, e.g., salary, benefits, remote work, travel, expense account, stock options, your boss, what projects you will be working on, etc.

Well, recruiting is the same. Once college coaches start recruiting you (meaning make DIRECT contact with you via phone in person), it's time for you to start evaluating them. You need to start considering questions such as:

- what are the facilities like;
- who are the coaches, and what are they like;
- who are the other players on the team, particularly in your position;
- what type of playing time can you expect;
- if you aspire to play professional baseball, what is the history of prior players making the jump;
- Is there any possibility of participating in a NIL program, etc., etc., etc?

You need to do your due diligence, e.g., visit the campus, talk to current players on the team, ask questions, and get answers to know what each school offers.

You also need to know where you stand with your academics. Will the coach be able to help with admissions? Have they pre-read your transcript, or will they know where you stand regarding admissibility? Do they have an idea of academic money?

In addition, you will need (at the D1 & 2 level) to go through the Initial

Academic Eligibility part of the NCAA, which determines that you have the proper grades in high school. These requirements change often, so visit the NCAA site or talk to your guidance counselor to ensure you are heading toward certification and are taking the proper steps.

When it comes to baseball scholarships, typically, the college coach will make his offer either after he gets an admission's read on you, maybe after you visit the school, or after he has seen you enough times to know you are worth the scholarship money.

You don't have to ask the college coach about baseball money; if they want to make an offer to you, they will. They can say the amount in a dollar figure or a percentage of the school's costs. Some put a short deadline on you to decide. Others give you longer. Everyone does their business a bit differently.

There are many other factors, too many for this chapter, to cover when it comes to scholarships, things such as what is or isn't negotiable, can your money go up or down, can you go from a non-scholarship player to a scholarship play while in college, how does NIL money factor in, what is required to keep your scholarship, and many other questions, but again these are things you should be asking the coach at the school who makes their offer.

The Decision

The last part of the process is deciding which of the schools is best for you. This can often be a challenging time for a young person, making what may likely be the most significant decision to date.

Generally speaking, if you have several schools you feel equally about, you can decide which is better academically, financially, or better for baseball.

My advice is to do a full visit of the school and see the dorms, the cafeteria, the classrooms, and the team in action to get a complete picture of what life is like at the school and whether you think you will fit in.

XII.   ProBatter Testimonials

"I just wish I'd had them when I was younger, there's nothing like it anywhere in the world! You can't beat it. You can change the length of it and the shape of it, all those features. I just think it's absolutely fantastic! And the replay is instantly there for you to watch on the TV screen, you know when your head is down or when your feet are down and all those sorts of things, so I just think there's nothing like it anywhere in the world. Well maybe we need it for Western Australia right now but there's no doubt in my mind that even the kid with an average amount of eye-hand coordination would develop tremendously."

Kim Hughes, Former Australia Cricket captain

****

"We just installed the ProBatter PX2 and the feedback has been wonderful, everyone loves it, and it is a great training tool!"

Bo Jackson, Bo Jackson's Elite Sports

****

"The ProBatter has already made these players better hitters. Price is a concern for college coaches but the ProBatter leasing program allowed us to fit in into our budget. The Program will also use it to produce revenue through camps, clinics and rentals."

Paul Kostacopoulos – Head Coach, US Naval Academy

****

"I love it. It's competitive and you have to compete against it to hit."

Alex Rodriguez – New York Yankees

****

"We've had a lot of success. It makes us feel great about what we do, especially when the parents can't afford it, and we have an opportunity for the kids to go to school and not have to pay anything. The technology has changed, and the guys love it."

Andy Concepcion, On Deck Baseball Academy - Las Vegas

****

"It greatly helped me to prepare for this past season as it could simulate game-like conditions. I can't get that from regular B.P. It was tremendous for situational hitting; placing myself in a 2-2 count against Clemens and then elevating a fastball or throwing a split."

Trot Nixon – Outfielder Boston Red Sox, Cleveland Indians

****

"This is better than a typical batting cage because this provides real-life real-time simulation this is just like being on the field facing a pitcher on the field and practicing a game situation versus just hitting a ball over and over and over out of a typical machine."

Robert, Owner of Peak Performance Training Center – Florida

****

"It's the most advanced training technology you can get to prepare hitters and catchers at any level whether it be you know a little league or whether they're getting ready to play pro ball. It's a system that allows it to have pinpoint accuracy consistently at every pitch. That takes kids to the next level and prepares them to be better than they've ever been. "It is as realistic a game as possible, it throws a variety of different pitches from fastball to curveball to change ups and with our instructions, there's no tool to get you better prepared for your season. So it's an awesome training tool!"

Jose Rijo Berger, Owner of Rijo Athletics

****

"It's the most realistic training device that's out there because it simulates game speed action from the pitcher's motion all the way through to the pitch coming through. It's perfect for the professionals - if their DHS has been sitting a while, this would be a perfect machine to warm him up."

Michael Lombardi, Director of West Side Training Center

****

"Pretty much if you can throw it on with a baseball you can throw it on this machine. We've got it anywhere from fastball curveball slider split righty lefty. You see pitchers out of the stretch, pitches out of the wind-up. If we want to throw the top right-hand inside corner to a righty, we can make it do that. If we want to throw a change-up down and away with a little bit of sinking action to the right, we can do that. This just gives us a chance to step back as instructors and watch as you hit live without having to focus on throwing pitches as well. We can concentrate on just solo While we're still getting the

realization of a real person throwing action. I felt like I became a much better hitter hitting off this machine, it's just nothing but a vast improvement on anything that has been around in my baseball career."
Charlie Lisk, Instructor at Gateway Grizzlies Baseball Academy

****

"The Probatter is extremely realistic from the wind up to the release point. You see the spin of the pitches that you can pick up. It actually is as close to a real game situation as I've ever seen. "One of the best things about the PX 3 is that it allows you to come in here in the privacy of your own batting cage or any batting cage and work on real baseball issues by yourself or with an individual coach."
Doug Vroman, Former Pro player, Hitting Instructor

****

"I like it because it's probably the most realistic pitching machine that I know of. Seeing the actual pitcher on the mound in the stretch or in the windup allows the batter to get its timing down."
Kelly Sharitt. NY Mets Minor League Organization

****

"This thing's just like being outside hitting off a real pitcher. The pitching that they face in here is better than any pitching that they'll face. It takes your learning curve and shrinks it. You learn from every at-bat so whatever level you're at, you can learn from each other, you're going to get better and that's what separates this from any other training tool."
Scott Vatter, Hit Streak Owner

****

"The ProBatter system is the best training tool I've ever seen. Many players just want to pound the ball. The simulator is great because it helps develop solid hitting fundamentals, with batters learning to make good contact."
Roy Burlison - National Softball Hall of Fame pitcher

****

"The Pinpoint control and wide range of pitches thrown by the ProBatter provides you with the chance to work on your hitting in game situations, which gives you the advantage you need to be a successful hitter."
Ron Krause Montreal Expos – Hitting instructor at Up to Bat

****

"We had the most success we ever had in the Florida Instructional league this fall with using the machine to teach our young hitters an approach to hitting a breaking pitch and the art of bunting for base hits. It was a huge help to our program."

Johnny Goryl – Assistant Director of Player Development – Cleveland Indians

* * * * * * * * * * * * * * *

"ProBatter has been a great addition to the experience here at Coors Field; and it has made my job easier. Our ProBatter game has been a workhorse. Zero down days last year. For a reliable and fun pitching game, call ProBatter."

Jason Fleming, Manager – Promotions Colorado Rockies

* * * * * * * * * * * * * *

"Everyone who steps in against the ProBatter system falls in love with it," "We have a huge number of competitive players in this area, and without a doubt, this is the best tool I've ever seen to help a player improve their hitting."

Sammy Carter – Co-Owner of On Deck Training Complex

* * * * * * * * * * * * * * * *

"To give players the best equipment in training on the mart out there. Plain and simple is the best thing since sliced bread. When you can throw that many pitches to different locations with accuracy, that speaks volumes." "I would take the machine home if I could."

Kurt Jaye – former owner of a California training facility

* * * * * * * * * * * * * * * *

"The ProBatter simulator is a tremendously versatile training tool. You can throw different pitches to different spots at different speeds but, you can do it on the fly with little adjustment or waiting time."

Brad Komminisk, ex-manager of the Kinston Indians

* * * * * * * * * * * * * * * *

"This is great for pitch recognition. We have been feeding our guys a heavy dose of breaking balls with the ProBatter system."

Lou Frazier – ex-coach – Columbus Red Stixx (Atlantic League)

* * * * * * * * * * * * * * * *

"I love this machine."

David Engle – Ex-Hitting Coach New York Mets

* * * * * * * * * * * * * * * *

"The ProBatter system is an ATM machine for my business. It's a great revenue generator."

Terry Hardtke, Hardke World of Baseball

****

"The ProBatter system worked great. It was in constant use by our prospects. One of the biggest advantages was to help our kids recognize breaking balls. It was the next best thing to big league pitching for them. In the beginning, our kids couldn't get near the ProBatter curve ball but after a few weeks, they were a lot more confident."

Mickey Brantley, ex-coach, N.Y. Mets

****

"The ProBatter machine affords hitters an opportunity to practice the game at full speed against Major League quality pitching and, unlike traditional pitching machines, to time the pitcher's delivery. The ProBatter machine is an important part of our hitting development program."

Ben Cherington – Director of Player Development Boston Red Sox

I have it in my hitting cages in Vegas...(Brain) Cashman called to ask me about it and I said it was great. It gives you a look at everything and at every speed."

Jason Giambi – New York Yankees

****

"Your machine is better than anyone could imagine. I was a 3rd round draft choice in 2005. I was a pitcher, but the Braves told me I would be playing outfield now. I went to the Gulf Coast League and hit .203 there. After thorough research I decided to buy your machine and I worked with it for 4 months and went back to play. That season I moved up two levels and hit .240. Last off season I worked with your machine again. This season I hit .312 in the two levels that I played in, made my first all-star team in pro ball and led all of minor league baseball with 176 total hits! I am so excited to get back to the off season so I can train with your machine. I am totally confident to tell you that your machine is helping me get to the big leagues! "

Jordan Shaffer, Atlanta Braves

****

"As we designed our new facility, we made a commitment to offer our customers the best of everything. We did extensive research and found that there's nothing else like the ProBatter PX2. The technology behind it is amazing. Hitting against the simulator is incredibly realistic and batters are given the unprecedented opportunity to train under near game conditions."

Chris Simon, co-owner of Sandlot Baseball & Softball Academy

* * * * * * * * * * * * * * * * * * * *

"We aim to provide every player who trains with us the very best training experience and the ProBatter PX2 is certainly the best tool for hitters. As a former player, I know there is no substitute to facing live pitching for a hitter to perfect his timing and rhythm. But it has been impossible to find one who can consistently and accurately throw over 90 mph – until now. ProBatter gives our students a tremendous opportunity to improve and take their game to the next level."

Mike Brooks, owner of West Coast Baseball Academy

* * * * * * * * * * * * * * * * * * * *

"The ProBatter system is exactly what our students need to improve their hitting," said Correa, who also serves as the academy's executive director. Every hitter has weaknesses, and the simulator allows the individual to work on the parts of his swing that need it the most. The machine is extremely accurate -- actually more precise than a human being -- and can deliver major league-quality pitches with great consistency. The improvement with hitters who train with the machine is dramatic."

Edwin Correa, owner Puerto Rico Baseball Academy and High School and former MLB Player

* *

"The ProBatter is the best way to train young hitters. Plus, it's been great for business."

Scott Burdick, Owner, All-American Training Center

* *

Appendix

ProBatter Product Catalog

A. ProBatter PX3 Baseball Video Pitching Simulator

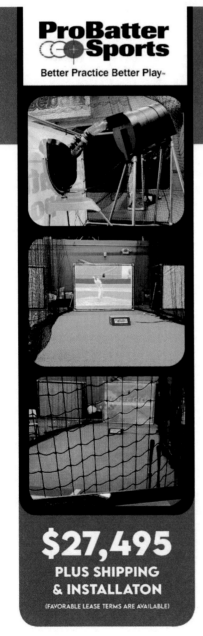

B. ProBatter PX3 Softball Video Pitching Simulator

C. ProBatter PX3 Cricket Video Bowling Simulator

ProBatter Sports
Better Practice Better Play™

ProBatter
The Ultimate Traning Tool for Hitters

PX3 CRICKET SIMULATOR

The ProBatter PX3 Cricket Video Simulator is the only one of its kind in the world and is used by a number of the top national teams and the ICC Training Center. Offered by the company that created the first video pitching simulators in 1999. The ProBatter PX3 Cricket Video Simulator is operated by a touch screen controller, the PX3 simulator contains a video production screen on which is projected the video image of a real-life cricket bowler whose timing is synchronized with the pitch head. It is capable of bowling at between 60 and 160 KPH. The PX3 simulator allows batters to experience game-like conditions resulting in improved timing, rhythm, and match performances.

The most popular features of the prior ProBatter generations have been retained, including:

- Fully programmable, user-friendly touchscreen controller
- Ability to interchangeably throw a variety of different pitches at speeds of 60 and 160 KPH
- Full-sized images of actual cricket bowlers
- Pinpoint accuracy
- Automatic feeder system available

While the programmable choices have been reduced from our top-of-the-line PX2 unit, the PX3 offers certain other advantag- es, including enhanced HD video quality and a self-contained kiosk for mounting the touchscreen controller all at a signifi- cantly reduced introductory price. We even offer as an option a ball tracking software product that can be integrated with the PX3.

For more information, Call 203-874-2500
49 Research Dr. Milford, CT 06460
info@probatter.com | www.ProBatter.com
LIKE US ON FACEBOOK @ ProBatter 2021

$27,495
PLUS SHIPPING & INSTALLATON
(FAVORABLE LEASE TERMS ARE AVAILABLE)

D.   ProBatter PX3 Combo Video Pitching Simulator

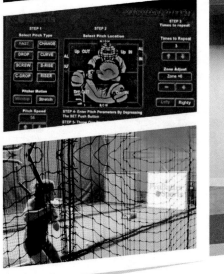

PROBATTER. PX3 "COMBO" PITCHING/ BOWLING VIDEO SIMULATOR

ProBatter's revolutionary new PX3 line of video simulators is the company's third generation of video simulators since it introduced its first one in 1999. Relying on cutting-edge technology and incorporating the lessons learned from the prior generations, the PX3 units combine the best features of the past with the advantages offered by present-day technology.

The PX3 "Combo" simulator is unique as it combines two different versions of PX3 simulators of your choice, such as baseball/softball or baseball/cricket, behind a projection screen. These simulators share a common controller and projection system, allowing customers to use the same tunnel for two different sports by simply switching from one version to the other with the touch of a button. Imagine the real estate you can save by being able to use a single tunnel for two different sports.

The PX3 "Combo" includes the following features:

- Two separately attached PX3 units mounted behind a common projection screen
- Ability to easily switch from one version to another
- Programmable, kiosk-mounted, touchscreen controller
- Ability to interchangeably throw a variety of different pitches from right-handed to left-handed pitchers/bowlers to multiple locations at speeds of 40-100 MPH
- Full-sized video images of actual pitchers
- Throws/bowls with pinpoint accuracy
- Includes an automatic feeder system

The PX3 "Combo" offers several advantages over earlier ProBatter "Combo" versions, most notably enhanced HD video quality, a superior projector, and an improved touchscreen controller. More importantly, at a price that is almost half the selling price of the PX2 "Combo," it is VERY AFFORDABLE. We even offer, as an added option, ball tracking software products such as Better Practice Better Play Hittrax or Rapsodo simulators that easily integrate with the "Combo."

For more information, Call 203-874-2500
49 Research Dr. Milford, CT 06460
info@probatter.com | www.ProBatter.com
LIKE US ON FACEBOOK @ ProBatter 2021

Better Practice Better Play~

E.   ProBatter PB II Video Conversion Kits

F. ProBatter Challenger Pitching Machine

G. ProBatter Strike Out Pro Pitcher Trainer

STRIKE OUT PRO
by ProBattersports®

WHAT IS IT?

Strike Out ProTM is a new, hi-tech pitching system that displays the video images of actual batters on a projection screen with portions of the strike zone highlighted as 'hot zones' for the pitcher to try to hit. Both right-hand- ed and left-handed batters can be displayed, and the hot zones can be varied from batter to batter using a wireless tablet. At the end of the session, the speed and accuracy of each pitch are displayed on the tablet. The system can even be pre-programmed to allow the pitcher to pitch a simulated game against a particular

FEATURES INCLUDE

- **CONTROLLED** - using a wireless tablet
- **ACCURATE** - precisely tracks pitch speeds and locations
- **LIFE-LIKE** - displays life-sized batters of all types
- **MULTIPLE TARGETS** - displays different zones to target
- **ANALYTICS** - records and stores data for analysis and development
- Catcher image moves to reflect different hot zones

WHO IS IT FOR

Strike Out Pro is ideal for pitcher training at all levels as well as for fan use at stadiums, amusement and entertainment venues.

For more information, Call 203-874-2500
49 Research Dr. Milford, CT 06460
info@probatter.com | www.ProBatter.com
LIKE US ON FACEBOOK

$14,995 PLUS SHIPPING & INSTALLATON

Contact Information

ProBatter Sports

Contact us at:

sales@probatter.com

203-874-2500

www.probatter.com

Index